Under the Ground

Rosemary Border

Oxford Bookworms
Factfiles

OXFORD UNIVERSITY PRESS 1996

Oxford University Press, Walton Street,
Oxford OX2 6DP

Oxford   New York
Athens   Auckland   Bangkok   Bombay
Calcutta   Cape Town   Dar es Salaam   Delhi
Florence   Hong Kong   Istanbul   Karachi
Kuala Lumpur   Madras   Madrid   Melbourne
Mexico City   Nairobi   Paris   Singapore
Taipei   Tokyo   Toronto

and associated companies in
Berlin   Ibadan

OXFORD and OXFORD ENGLISH
are trade marks of Oxford University Press

ISBN 0 19 422807 X

© Oxford University Press

First published 1996

No unauthorized photocopying

Printed in Hong Kong

OXFORD BOOKWORMS

For a full list of titles in all the Oxford Bookworms
series, please refer to the Oxford English catalogue.

Factfiles
Original readers giving varied and interesting informa-
tion about a range of non-fiction topics. Titles available
include:

Stage 1 (400 headwords)
New York *John Escott*
London *John Escott*
Animals in Danger *Andy Hopkins and Joc Potter*

Stage 2 (700 headwords)
Football *Steve Flinders*
Rainforests *Rowena Akinyemi*
Under the Ground *Rosemary Border*

Stage 3 (1000 headwords)
Recycling *Rosemary Border*
The Cinema *John Escott*

Black Series
Original stories and adaptations of classic and modern
fiction.

Green Series
Adaptations of classic and modern stories for younger
readers.

Oxford Bookworms Collection
Fiction by well known classic and modern authors. Texts
are not abridged or simplified in any way.

ACKNOWLEDGEMENTS

The publishers would like to thank the following for
permission to reproduce photographs:

Ancient Art & Architecture/Ronald Sheridan pp. 1, 8

Ardea/Ian Beames p. 15, John Daniels p. 15, P. Morris p. 7

Eurotunnel p. 16

Eye Ubiquitous/Simon Arnold p. 15, Bob Gibbons p. 3,
John Miles p. 18, J B Pickering p. 17

Hulton Deutsch/Haywood Magee pp. 12, 13

Mary Evans pp. 10, 14

Natural History Museum p. 9

Oxford Scientific Films Survival Anglia/Frances Furlong
p. 6, Mike Linley p. 7, John De Meester Okapia p. 16,
Dieter and Mary Plage p. 7

Stock House Limited/Ken Straiton p. 19

Times Newspapers Limited p. 18

Tony Waltham pp. 2, 3, 5, 11, 13

1 Lost – and found!

The boys could see wonderful things

In 1940 five boys were walking with their dog in the hills near Lascaux in France. Suddenly the dog fell down a hole in the ground. He was not hurt, but the boys could not touch him because the hole was too narrow. They moved some stones away from the hole to widen it. 'I think there's a cave under here!' said one of the boys. 'Good boy!' he called to the dog. 'We're coming!'

One by one, they went down through the hole into the cave.

'It's dark in here! Has anybody got a light?' One boy had a box of matches. By their light the boys could see wonderful things. Pictures of animals covered the walls and roof of the cave. The boys were very surprised to find these bright, new paintings under a hill near their homes. Then the last match went out and the cave was dark again. The boys helped their dog out of the cave and hurried home to tell the news.

The boys did not know, but the paintings were many thousands of years old. You can read more about the caves of Lascaux on page 9.

2   All about caves

There are many different kinds of caves. Some caves have been there for millions of years, but many are only a few thousand years old. Most caves are natural – nobody made them – but some caves are artificial – they were made by people.

Some caves are even smaller than a small room, but some are hundreds of kilometres long. The most interesting ones have many large and small 'rooms' (called chambers) with wide and narrow passages between them. They have underground rivers and waterfalls too.

Most natural caves were made thousands of years ago by rain water, and a soft grey or white stone called limestone. Limestone is special in two ways. First, limestone contains many cracks and holes. Second, when rain water and air touch limestone, they dissolve it.

Ogof Ffynnon Ddu Cave, Wales

Stalagmites

When rain falls on a hillside, the water runs down into the small cracks and holes in the stone. It dissolves the stone and slowly widens the cracks. Then it runs along under the ground and carries the dissolved limestone with it.

Sometimes drops of water, full of dissolved limestone, fall through the soft stone into a cave underneath. The limestone hardens again. Slowly, many strange and beautiful shapes are made.

In some caves there are natural stone bridges across underground rivers which dried up thousands of years ago. There are great waterfalls of stone. There are strange shapes like trees and flowers. The most famous shapes are stalactites and stalagmites. Stalactites come down from the roof of the cave. Stalagmites come up from the floor. When a stalagmite and a stalactite meet, they make a column. Some chambers are so full of columns that they look like churches. Most of these shapes are the same colour as the limestone of the cave, but not always. If the water contains metal, the shapes can be many different colours.

Looking up at stalactites

A curtain of stalactites

3 Caves of the world

Many countries across the world have no caves. This is not because there are no mountains in those places. Some of the world's biggest mountains have no caves – they are not made of limestone. But the low limestone hills of the north of England and the south of France are full of interesting caves.

For hundreds of years people have enjoyed finding caves and going down inside them. This sport is called caving, and the people who do it are called cavers. The first cavers were in Europe, and most cavers still live there.

That is why we know a lot about European caves.

But in other parts of the world there are hundreds of caves which very few people have ever visited. For example, there are many caves in Russia and Afghanistan, Albania and China, but there are not many cavers in those countries and it is often very difficult for foreign cavers to visit their caves.

The deepest cave that we know about is the 1535 metre Gouffre Jean Bernard in France, but perhaps there are caves which are

Caves around the world

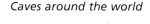

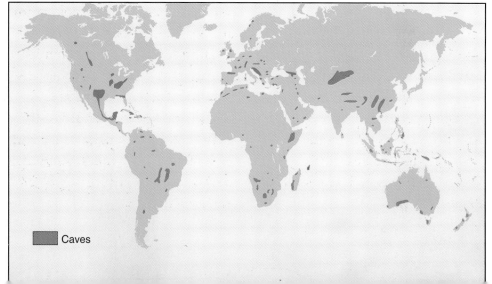

Caves

The Big Room, Carlsbad Caverns

deeper. And the longest cave we know about today is the Mammoth Cave in the USA, which has more than 474 kilometres of passages. There is nothing small about Mammoth Cave. Many cave passages are very low and narrow, but some of the biggest passages in Mammoth Cave are ten metres tall! But perhaps in China or Indonesia there are higher and longer caves.

Where is the world's most beautiful cave? That is a difficult question, because every caver has a favourite. If you are looking for a cave which is both big and beautiful, visit the Big Room in the Carlsbad Caverns in the USA. The Big Room is a natural underground chamber. It is 100 metres high, 200 metres wide and 300 metres long, and it is full of wonderful stalactites and stalagmites.

4   Life underground

Caves are dark – *really* dark. You cannot see your hand in front of your face. Green plants cannot live without light; so the only trees and flowers under the ground are made of stone. But there *are* living things in caves. Some kinds of plant (called fungi), which do not need light, live there. Air and water carry other, very small, animals and plants into the cave. These animals and plants are food for bigger animals. And two animals bring light into the cave too.

Glow-worms in Waitomo Cave

Glow-worms

One of these animals is Man. The other is a small animal called a glow-worm, which lives in some caves. The Waitomo Cave in New Zealand is never dark; there are thousands of glowing lights from these little worms which cover the roof of the cave. Why do glow-worms glow? Nobody knows!

Caves are always cold, but in winter they are much warmer than outside. So some animals come into caves for their winter sleep. Other animals sleep and make their nests in caves, but go outside to catch their food.

Many millions of bats live in caves all over the world. Most bats are quite small and catch flies to eat, but others are very big and eat fruit. Some people think bats cannot see, but this is not true. Bats have eyes, but they do not always use them. They can fly about very well in the dark, because they make noises which hit the walls and the roof of the cave. The bats hear these noises, and they know where they are.

Some birds make their nests in caves and fly out every evening to look for food.

There are underground fish too. When they are born, the young fish have eyes. As they get bigger, their eyes get smaller and skin begins to cover them. After about seven weeks, you cannot see their eyes at all. These fish do not need eyes because there is nothing to see in their dark caves. They have a lot of small hairs on their skin. These hairs feel things and help them to find food.

The most interesting cave animal is the white underground salamander. The salamander, which is usually about thirty centimetres long, has no eyes, but like the fish it feels things through its skin. It does not need much to eat and can live for a year or more without food.

A white Salamander

Bats in a cave

Bats flying

5 Cave people

Hundreds of thousands of years ago, before people started to build houses, a dry cave was a safe place to live. Daylight came in through the mouth of the cave and they could make a fire there to keep animals away.

Today you can still find burnt wood, broken tools and pieces of animal bone from the cave people's meals; and in a limestone cave near Peking in China in 1921, cavers found the bones of a cave man who died 500,000 years ago.

Cave people painted pictures and made models of animals too. Nobody really knows why they did this, but we can think of possible answers. We know they wanted to catch the real animals, eat their meat and use their skins for clothes. Today, some people keep a picture of a person or thing that they love or want, and look at the

A stone tool

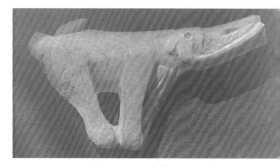

A cave model

picture of it every day ('One day I'll have a car/house/wife like that'). And a few people make models of somebody that they do not like, then 'hurt' the model.

Cave models are not always very beautiful; but cave paintings are so wonderful that at first many people were sure that they were modern. In Altamira in Spain in 1868, a man found a cave with stone tools on the floor and many beautiful paintings of animals. For many years, everybody said the paintings were 'too good' to be the work of cave people. Now we know that they are about seventeen thousand years old.

We do not usually find pictures or models in the parts of the cave where people lived and worked. Nearly all cave paintings and models are in the deepest, darkest, most secret places. That is why they were lost for thousands of years.

Too many visitors

Soon after the boys (and their lost dog) found the caves of Lascaux, thousands of people came to see the wonderful paintings there. Then the problems started.

Green plants need light; that is why the only green plants in a cave are near the cave mouth. But visitors to the Lascaux caves needed artificial light to see the paintings. Soon small green plants covered the walls and roof – and the paintings too. In 1967 the caves were closed, while people looked for an answer to the problem. After many years a visitors' centre was built. There people can see an artificial cave which is just like the real one in every way.

In 1994, three cavers found another painted cave in France. The paintings at Chauvet-Pont-d'Arc are older than Lascaux and Altamira, and they are very beautiful. This cave will never be a show cave. 'We made too many mistakes at Lascaux,' says a French caver.

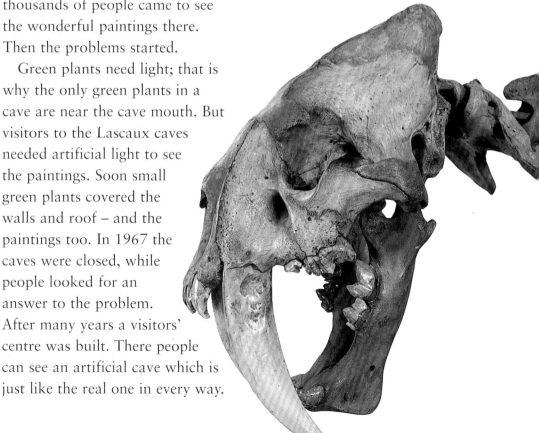

Bones from a sabre-toothed cat which lived 15,000 years ago

6 Going underground

Caving seventy years ago

Why do people go caving? It is always dark, usually dirty, often difficult and sometimes dangerous. A caver says:

'You push yourself down through a narrow crack in the hill side. Usually you have to go down a rope. Sometimes you swim through deep water. You pull yourself along through narrow passages only fifty centimetres high, then suddenly you're in a chamber as big as a church.

'It's always midnight underground, until *you* make it light. Then you see wonderful things – stalactites, stalagmites columns, shining waterfalls and bridges of many-coloured stone. Perhaps you are the first person to see them – every year, cavers find many new chambers and passages. When you leave, you take your light with you and the cave is dark and silent again.'

Long ago, cavers went underground in their ordinary clothes. Their only light came from candles. Most cavers today wear one-piece suits in bright colours. They wear 'hard hats' with lamps which burn for many hours. They carry special radios and very strong ropes.

Sometimes cavers have to swim through water. Then special 'wet suits' keep them warm and dry.

There are many show caves which people can visit without getting dirty or wet. People widen the passages and make floors and stairs. They put in artificial light to show the most beautiful shapes.

Caving today

A show cave in China

7   Down the mine

A mine is a place where people take something out of the ground. All over the world, people have mined for coal, metal and stone for thousands of years.

Sometimes miners find caves by accident when they are looking for metal or stone. Sometimes they are looking for something ordinary, and find something special. An example is the beautiful blue-purple stone called Blue John. Miners found Blue John when they were looking for metal. Visitors to the Treak Cliff Caves in the north west of England can see the biggest and most expensive piece of Blue John in the world. Nobody can take it away, because it is a natural column 1.8 metres thick and it holds up the roof of a big cave with beautiful, colourful stalactites and stalagmites.

Coal mines long ago were terrible places. Horses, men, women and children worked underground. Men pulled themselves along through narrow passages to cut the coal by hand. Horses pulled heavy trucks full of coal along narrow underground railways. The horses lived in underground stables and never saw the sun. Women and children carried bags of coal or pulled trucks in passages which were too narrow for horses.

In modern coal mines, machines do most of the work. But in some countries, women and children – and horses – still work underground.

Pulling a coal truck

Not all miners used trucks. More than two hundred years ago the metal miners in Speedwell Cavern in England used boats on an artificial waterway called a canal. The mine closed long ago but the canal is still there, deep underground. The mine is now a museum and visitors can ride along the canal in small boats.

Speedwell Cavern

Many other mines are museums now. Visitors put on hard hats and lamps and go down a real mine a hundred metres underground. At Big Pit coal mine in Wales, visitors see the underground lamp rooms, tool rooms and stables. They also see the baths, which the miners paid for themselves, in 1936. Before then, they had to wash at home in a small metal bath in front of the fire.

A coal miner fify years ago

Clearwell in the west of England is a natural cave which is also a mine. A hundred years ago, men, women and children went through narrow cracks with candles in their mouths and 30 kilos of stone and metal on their backs. Today Clearwell, too, is an underground museum. Sometimes there are special visits to the deep parts of the mine. Visitors put on hard hats with lamps and go through the narrow, stony passages like the miners of long ago.

8 Under the city

Engineers have made mines and tunnels underground for thousands of years. A tunnel is an artificial passage under the ground or under the water. Many tunnels carry railways, canals and roads under hills and fields; but some of the most interesting tunnels are under city streets. Some are still used; and some are silent and empty.

The London Underground in 1883

There have been many changes since the world's first underground railway was built in London almost 150 years ago. Old lines have closed and new ones have opened; and London has many dark, empty underground stations. They do things better in Paris. As trains hurry through one empty underground station, passengers see a 50 metre painting of a sunny beach. 'It makes me think of my summer holidays!' said one passenger.

In London, letters travel by underground railway. The 'Mail Rail' was built in 1927 and is still working beautifully. There are no passengers and no drivers. The 'Mail Rail' carries 23,000 bags of mail every day. The letters travel quickly and miss London's traffic problems.

Every city has sewers under its streets to carry away the sewage from bathrooms everywhere. Before the London sewers were built, everything went into the River Thames. The water was thick and brown; no fish could live in it. By 1858 nobody could work in the new Houses of Parliament because of the smell.

The great engineer Joseph Bazalgette built hundreds of kilometres of new sewers under London. Many are still used today. Narrow sewers carry the sewage into wider ones, then underground rivers of sewage run through great tunnels.

It is possible to walk through the sewers, but there are also TV cameras on wheels which travel along the sewers and send pictures. When something goes wrong, engineers send machines along the sewer. But sometimes a person has to do the job.

There are millions of rats in sewers all over the world. There are many stories of stranger animals too – and a few of these

Roman sewers built 2,000 years ago

are true. In 1984 workers found a baby crocodile in a sewer and a Swedish family found a snake in their toilet. 'People buy animals then, when they get tired of them, they put them down the toilet,' says an engineer. 'Our workers often see goldfish swimming along. And we sometimes see terrapins too.'

A rat

A terrapin

9 Tunnels

Some wild animals, like moles, are natural tunnellers. Long ago, people also learned to tunnel to enlarge natural caves.

Some tunnels were built to carry people. The oldest tunnel for travellers was built four thousand years ago under the river Euphrates. The Romans were great tunnellers. Many of their tunnels brought water to towns or fields, or carried sewage away. The Romans tunnelled through thousands of metres of rock. They used fire and water – fire to make the rock hot, then water to make it cold. The sudden change of temperature cracked the rock. Later, engineers found easier ways of breaking up the rock. One of these was a machine called a mole!

Tunnels make journeys shorter. The first railway tunnel under the Alps, the high mountains between Italy and France, was the 14 kilometre Mont Cenis Tunnel (1857 to 1871).

A mole tunnelling

The Channel Tunnel

A road tunnel in the Alps

Road tunnels under the mountains are more difficult to build than railway tunnels. You need to bring clean air into the tunnel, and you need to take bad air out. The 11.25 kilometre Mont Blanc Tunnel between Italy and France was a difficult, dangerous job which gave the engineers a lot of problems. They started on both sides of the mountain in 1959 and met in the middle in 1962. Now a million drivers use the tunnel every year. It shortens the journey between Paris and Rome by 200 kilometres.

Tunnelling under the sea

The world's longest under-sea tunnel is the Seikan Tunnel between the Japanese islands of Honshu and Hokkaido. It is 54 kilometres long. It took 42 years to plan and build, and it opened in 1988. But perhaps the most interesting under-sea tunnel is the 50 kilometre Channel Tunnel between England and France, because tunnelling started four times and stopped three times!

Work started in 1877, 1881 and 1975. In 1987 tunnelling started again, and this time the engineers finished the job. Now special trains take passengers and cars through the tunnel.

10   At home underground

There are still some people who live underground. A few do so because they do not know any other way of life. The Tasaday people of the Philippine Islands, for example, have always lived in caves.

Some people live underground because they want to. The Duke of Portland lived almost two hundred years ago. He already had a great house called Welbeck Abbey. But he built a church, stables, living rooms and kitchens – all under the ground. Between the buildings he made many underground passages. The longest is more than a kilometre long and goes under a lake in the garden. Welbeck Abbey is now a school for young soldiers and nobody goes into the Duke's underground buildings.

In Japan land is very expensive. So in the 1980s people started to build underground. Now Tokyo has four kilometres of underground streets with underground shops and

The tunnel to the kitchens, Welbeck Abbey

At home in Coober Pedy

restaurants. Osaka has an underground shopping city with a river, a waterfall and a small lake with real flowers and artificial birds. Now Japanese engineers are planning great underground cities called geodomes. They are already building the first geodome near Tokyo. There are underground streets in Canada too. In Canada the winters are very cold. People can walk to work safely when there is deep snow in the streets above their heads.

Coober Pedy is in a very hot, dry part of Australia. The name comes from an old Australian word which means 'White Man's Tunnel'. The town has 800 underground houses and 600 houses above ground. There are underground shops, garages, hotels, churches and a book shop called (naturally) Underground Books. Why do the Coober Pedy people live underground? The answer is the weather.

In summer the temperature in the day time is often 35 to 47 degrees Celsius. At night in winter,

Underground shops in Japan

the temperature is often only one or two degrees. Under the ground the temperature is never higher than 26 degrees and never lower than 20 degrees.

Wooden columns hold up the stone roofs of the underground houses. The stone is sometimes a beautiful golden colour.

Some people think that underground homes are the answer to many problems. There are some underground houses in Europe already. Perhaps one day there will be underground towns all over the world.

Exercises

A Checking your understanding

Pages 1–5 *How much can you remember? Check your answers.*
1 What were the boys doing before they found the cave at Lascaux?
2 What does water do to limestone?
3 What is the difference between a stalactite and a stalagmite?
4 Where is the deepest cave that we know about?

Pages 6–9 *Are these sentences true (T) or false (F)?*
1 Nobody knows why glow-worms glow.
2 Underground salamanders need a lot of food.
3 The caves at Lascaux are closed, but visitors can see artificial caves which are just like the real ones.
4 There is a new cave in France which will soon be open to visitors.

Pages 10–13 *Choose the right words.*
1 Long ago, cavers' light came from matches/candles/lights on their hats.
2 Blue John is a miner/a famous caver/a blue-purple stone.
3 In the Speedwell Cavern the miners carried metal in boats/in trucks/on their backs.

Pages 14–17 *Write answers to these questions.*
1 Where is there an underground railway with no drivers?
2 Why do workers sometimes find unusual animals in sewers?
  Who built the London sewers?
4 How did Roman engineers break up hard rock?
5 When was the first railway tunnel under the Alps built?

Pages 18–19 *How much can you remember? Check your answers.*
1 What is special about Osaka's underground shopping city?
2 What does Coober Pedy mean?
3 What is the name of the bookshop at Coober Pedy?

B Working with Language

1 *Use these words to make these ten short sentences into five longer ones. You can use one of the words more than once.*

because   when   and   but

1 The last match went out. The cave was dark again.
2 Some caves have been there for millions of years. Many are only a few thousand years old.
3 Some miners find caves. They are looking for metal or stone.
4 Bats can fly very well in the dark. They make noises which help them to know where they are.
5 In Canada people can walk to work safely. There is deep snow in the streets above their heads.

2 *Put these sentences into the right order. Then check your answers on page 16.*

1 They used fire and water to crack the rock.
2 The Romans were great tunnellers and tunnelled through thousands of metres of rock.
3 Later, engineers used a machine called a mole.
4 Thousands of years ago, people learned to enlarge natural caves.
5 Some animals, like moles, are natural tunnellers.

C Activities

1 Imagine you are one of the boys who found the Lascaux caves. What did you see and how did you feel?
2 Have you ever been into a cave or mine? What can you remember about it?

D Project Work

Find out about a cave, tunnel or mine near your home. Write a short guide to it.

Glossary

coal black, hard wood from trees which died millions of years ago

crack (n) a long, narrow hole

crack (v) to make a crack

dissolve to break up in water – for example, sugar dissolves in water

duke an important man with a lot of land and (usually) a lot of money

fell past tense of 'to fall'

found past tense of 'to find'

lost past tense of 'to lose'

mail letters, etc. which people send to each other

match a small piece of wood with a special end which starts to burn when you hit it against its special box

mine a place where people get coal and metals out of the ground

museum a place where people can look at and learn about things from a long time ago

nest a home which many birds and some animals build

passage a way between two rooms

roof the top part of a cave or building

rope a long line which people use for pulling things, and for climbing

sewage dirty water, etc.

sewer an underground passage for dirty water from bathrooms and toilets

skin the all-over covering of the body

temperature how hot or cold something or someone is